All Shall

Prophesy

A 30-Day Prophetic Devotional

RON CAMPBELL

with *New York Times* bestselling author

RON BRACKIN

Cover Art: Chris Gifford

The testimony of Jesus is the spirit of prophecy.[1]

[1] Revelation 19:10, NKJV.

introduction

PROPHECY is the voice of Love in the mouths of his beloved— his heart expressed to and through our spirit.

Prophecy preceded time. God prophesied heavens and earth, light, land and animals for a man. And we became.

Since Pentecost, God has poured out his Spirit completely on all who have given themselves to him, enabling us all to prophesy.[2]

And all we need is a yearning heart and listening ears.[3]

---

[2] Acts 2:18.

[3] The *Prophetic Path 101* online course is now available at www.propheticacademy.com.

day 1

In the very beginning, the Living Expression was already there.[4]

AMONG all your other identities, you are The Prophet. From your place outside of time, you prophesied time and a world and an ever-expanding universe. Then, you declared them, and they became.

So it seems to me that prophecy is a lot more than words of wisdom and knowledge.

You said once through Balaam (when he was in the Spirit and not peddling omens), that prophets are people whose eyes see clearly the purpose and will of God, who hear the words of God and who see the vision of the Almighty.[5]

That can't mean that only super-saints can prophesy. Biblical prophets were flawed too.

---

[4] John 1:1.
[5] Numbers 24:1-4, AMP.

To make things even more confusing, you said that, ever since Pentecost, *all* who love you can prophesy,[6] which can be a little scary, because prophecy comes across as one of your most unusual and mysterious gifts.

I mean, even if I understood prophecy, how can I tell whether a voice in my head is yours or a memory of something I read or a comment I heard on TV? Or what if it's a demon's voice?

I have questions.

Nevertheless, you seem to have important things you want to say through me prophetically.

So, please, teach me more.

---

[6] Acts 2:17-18.

day 2

*"[T]rust in God stems from understanding
His character, not His reasons."[7]*

I get a kick out of husbands and
wives who finish each other's
sentences. It doesn't seem rude. It
seems like they're joined at the head
and share one another's thoughts. They
don't necessarily agree on everything,
but they don't try to manipulate each
other. They just seem to feel safe with
one another.

It would be wonderful to be like
that with you, Lord, to share your
thoughts and to always trust you.

Prophets seem to do that. I mean I
think it takes an awful lot of trust for
anyone to say in public that they're
speaking for God.

What if I'm wrong?

What if I'm influenced by events or
emotions or moods or lunch? What if

[7] Piper, Barnabas, *Help My Unbelief*, The Good Book
Company, 1 January 2020.

I tell someone to sell their house and move or quit their job or give away an inheritance?

I guess that's where the trust kicks in. Prophets trust that, if they're wrong, if they make a mistake, you won't open the earth and swallow them up or cause them to spontaneously combust.

And if some people misuse, misunderstand or ignore a word they're given, well, that's between them and you.

It helps me to understand that.

Prophecy can be terrifying. But when it is, it's because I've got my eyes on me and my image and my reputation, deluding me into thinking that I'm more important than what you have to say through me.

Help me get over that. Help me to trust you more and value myself less.

day 3

[W]hen we live God's way, He brings gifts into our lives, much the same way that fruit appears in an orchard—things like affection for others, exuberance about life, serenity. We develop a willingness to stick with things, a sense of compassion in the heart, and a conviction that a basic holiness permeates things and people. We find ourselves involved in loyal commitments, not needing to force our way in life, able to marshal and direct our energies wisely.[8]

WHENEVER I pass some place that's featuring a prophet, I know the parking lot will soon overflow with people who want to know their future. But is that what prophecy is really about?

Your prophets aren't psychic readers or fortunetellers, showmen or media personalities.

Reminding myself that you've called us all to prophesy, it seems that we

---

[8] Galatians 5:22, MSG.

should put more effort into growing fruit than telling fortunes.

John Paul Jackson wrote that "Godly character is of greater value than spiritual giftedness."[9]

I mean, if I'm speaking for you, I'm representing you. And how can I imagine I'm representing you without manifesting love and peace, patience and kindness, goodness, faithfulness, gentleness and self-control?

The thought of speaking for you overwhelms me—that you would trust me with your words, trust me to affect the life of someone you love.

Help me keep my eyes and my heart focused on yours, Lord.

---

[9] Jackson, John Paul, The Art of Hearing God, Revised Sixth Edition, Streams Institute for Spiritual Development, 2010, p. 3.

day 4

If I had the gift of prophecy and knew all about what is going to happen in the future, knew everything about everything, but didn't love others, what good would it do?[10]

THERE'S that love thing again. Okay, here's the way it looks from where I'm sitting. When I prophesy, I'm speaking for you. You're Love.[11] So I can only speak properly for you out of love, right? And even loving words can be angry.

But love has become a tricky word. It's used these days to describe so much that it no longer describes much of anything. Golf, gold or God. I love 'em all. So what does love mean? Especially when love is the only word in the entire Bible that comes after the words "God is."

---

[10] 1 Corinthians 13:2, TLB.
[11] 1 John 4:8.

7

Love is the force that empowers me to forgive people who hurt me or hurt those closest to me.

Love is the strength that enables me to endure loss.

Love is your character, so why wouldn't it be the character growing in your prophets?

If you are love, it seems to me that to be without love is to be without you. And what valid, strengthening, healing, correcting or directing words am I likely to receive in this self-centered world apart from you?

Love is the heart of the prophetic, the validation of the prophetic and the power of the prophetic.

You sent the prophetic into the world, not to repair the world or to impress the world, but to prepare the world for your soon return.

Teach me to hear you accurately, to hear your heart as well as your voice.

day 5

The source of revelation-knowledge is found as you fall down in surrender before the Lord. Don't expect to see Shekinah glory until the Lord sees your sincere humility.[12]

JUST about everybody seems to be proud these days. Instead of one of the "Seven Deadly Sins," Pride has become a sought-after modern virtue.

Humility, on the other hand, doesn't seem to be valued much at all in my if-ya-got-it-flaunt-it world.

I think Pride has taken down more of your people than even Lust. And your prophets seem to be among Pride's prime targets.

Little wonder, though.

Your children flock to them and press in around them like a crowd of silly girls around a rock star. We follow prophets and hang on their every word, hoping one of the words will be for us.

---

[12] Proverbs 15:33, TPT.

9

The trick to prophesying seems to be a constant awareness that the word is coming *from* you *through* me, which makes me about as important as a megaphone.

I should probably memorize the story of Balaam[13] to help me remember that you can prophesy through any old donkey.

One more thought about humility.

When I summon up the courage to speak a prophetic word, I get it wrong from time to time. How that affects me will depend on how I see you.

The more my eyes are fixed on me, the smaller and meaner I appear.

The more I fix my eyes on you, the nearer and dearer you appear.

Help me live more of my life face to face with you, Lord.

---

[13] Numbers 22.

day 6

Spiritual formation in Christ moves toward a total interchange of our ideas and images for his.[14]

ACCORDING to Jeff Zacks, a professor of psychology and brain sciences, "Memory isn't for trying to remember. It's for doing better next time."[15]

That would mean I can make myself better later by comparing myself now to myself before.

But that makes me all about me—before, now and always.

The only way to make myself better is to compare myself to you.

And there's no better place to learn about you than in the Bible. I just have to remember that I come with baggage and deal with that when I get there.

---

[14] Willard, Dallas, *Renovation of the Heart*, NavPress, 2002.

[15] Everding-Wustl, Gerry, "How memories shape ideas about our present and future," *Futurity*, 30 July 2018.

If I expect the Bible to be academic—telling me about olden folks, olden days and olden ways in the Middle East—that's all I'll see. Same thing if I'm just looking for verses to memorize and recite. Same thing if I use your Word mostly as a reference book.

I need to keep in mind that your Word is alive.

Your voice in Scripture tunes prophetic ears, reconfigures prophetic minds, breaks prophetic hearts and makes them beat as one with yours.

How can I prophesy without knowing how and what you think? And how can I possibly know how and what you think without hanging out with you, talking with you, watching you, listening to you?

These, of course, are rhetorical questions.

day 7

God is going to reveal me as a flawed human being as fast as he can, and he's going to enjoy it because it will force me to grapple with real intimacy."[16]

INTIMACY with you reveals our secret stuff, the stuff that will never see daylight if we have anything to say about it. The silly thing about that is we think we can hide the stuff from you as well.

So sometimes you use prophets like x-ray machines to expose the deepest stuff. Not publicly, of course, because you're Love, and your objective is to heal and liberate, not to embarrass or shame.

The prophetic is intolerant of pretense because it separates us from you. Your arms are open wide, eager to embrace me as I truly am, rather than as I think you want me to be. But you

---

[16] Miller, Donald, *Scary Close: Dropping the Act and Finding True Intimacy*, Thomas Nelson, 10 February 2015.

can't because I'm posing as someone I'm not. Prophecy removes my barriers.

You also send your prophets to re-pave the ways of intimacy with you. Redirecting churches that have drifted from you. Reverting them to organisms instead of organizations. Repeating their calling to meet needs and not just meet.

Mostly, though, we pursue intimacy with you. Not with our hands out and gimme-gimmes gushing from our mouths, but stretched out, face to the floor, terrified and humbled by our growing awareness of your love.

Prophets learn to stay connected, which just requires an open line.

When things interrupt us, I don't want to hang up. I want to just step away, take care of it and come back to you.

day 8

Mistakes aren't a necessary evil. They aren't evil at all. They are an inevitable consequence of doing something new.[17]

NONE of us are spiritually mature when we're born again. Shortly after we get here, we have poopy diapers, just like we did when we were born physically.

And the mess continues when you start to give me prophetic words to share. I can't be sure I'm right, because I can't see you or talk it over first. You say something, and your voice sounds pretty much the same in my head as my voice or my imagination or the devil's voice, for that matter.

So one of the first things I learn is that prophetic words are more a matter of content than tone and perceived by my spirit instead of my ears.

---

[17] Catmull, Ed, *Creativity, Inc.*, Random House, 8 April 2014.

This is a whole new thing. And it's a little scary at first. Mostly because I'm afraid of embarrassing myself more than embarrassing you. I mean, you're God, but I have a reputation to protect.

That logic, of course, is a child's logic. I need to get over it and practice fixing my eyes on you more than on the people around me.

I need to understand that prophecy is divine and supernatural and lots better than fortunetelling.

But it takes time and practice, like learning to ride a bike, read a book or walk a tightrope above a canyon on a breezy day.

Yup, it's risky, but mostly to my ego. And what a tiny price to pay for hearing from and speaking for you!

A man who is held in honor, yet who lacks spiritual understanding and a teachable heart, is like the beasts that perish.[18]

WE all start out in life with teachable hearts. I was learning in my mother's womb before I took my first breath.[19] After I was born, I learned in school, in play, in fights, in relationships.

My heart was always wide open.

But I wasn't born with spiritual understanding. I didn't get it in school. I didn't get it even by reading your Bible. I got it when I gave you my life. And suddenly, BOOM! There it was.

I didn't get it all at once, though.

It's came bit by bit, depending mostly on the depth of our relationship, which is not merely an issue of time—putting in more hours

---

[18] Psalm 49:20, AMP.
[19] Skwarecki, Beth, "Babies Learn to Recognize Words in the Womb, *Science Mag*, 26 August 2013.

reading the Bible, praying or worshiping and putting it all in context. A tool is worthless unless it's used, tried and proved.

It's not just setting aside an hour a day. It's a matter of keeping myself aware of your presence throughout all my distractions and duties and pushing through things that would separate us.

A lot of people wonder how that works, how they make it happen. But I don't think I'm *making* it happen.

My focus isn't on moving closer. I'm not particularly aware of the distance between us. My focus is simply on you.

The closer we get to one another and the more I learn about you, the more I want to learn and the more desperately I feel my need for you.

day 10

You do not question an author who appears on the title page as "T.V.N. Persaud, M.D., Ph.D., D.Sc., F.R.C.Path. (Lond.)."[20]

PROPHECY is a gift, not a skill, and a prophet is a servant, not a title.

Prophecy is not my words. It's your presence in me and you passing through me.

"For prophecy never had its origin in the human will, but prophets, though human, spoke from God as they were carried along by the Holy Spirit."[21]

The incredible joy of prophecy is not flourishing a divine gift in an overflowing church or auditorium. The joy is you, so close to me that I hear you whispering in my ear.

---

[20] Roach, Mary, *Stiff: The Curious Lives of Human Cadavers,* W.W. Norton & Company, 17 May 2004.
[21] 1 Peter 1:21.

So many times, when you give me something to pass on, I'm so thrilled that you spoke through me that I totally miss the heart-pounding experience of being so close to you. I can get so focused on me that I miss you entirely, and "prophet" becomes nothing more than a title.

While prophecy brings me closer to you, it also brings you closer to your church.

"It is good," Paul said, "that you are enthusiastic and passionate about spiritual gifts especially prophecy....

"When someone prophesies, he speaks to encourage people, to build them up, and to bring them comfort....the one who prophesies builds up the church."[22]

Mostly, though, prophecy puts your words in my mouth and binds my heart more closely to yours.

---

[22] 1 Corinthians 14:1, 3, 4, TPT.

day 11

"Honest to God, Bill, the way things are going, all I can think of is that I'm a character in a book by somebody who wants to write about somebody who suffers all the time."[23]

WE don't talk much about suffering these days, except to complain.

We don't care for the idea that you allow it to heal and strengthen us or that, in our fallen world, suffering just *is*.

We love to think about Joseph becoming Pharaoh's number two. But to get from his flock to his fortune, he had to be "sold as a slave. His feet were bruised by strong shackles and his soul was held by iron."

Your promise to Joseph "purged his character until it was time for his dreams to come true."[24]

---

[23] Vonnegut, Kurt, *Breakfast of Champions*, Dial Press Trade Paperback, 11 May 1999.
[24] Psalm 105:16-19, TPT.

Paul suffered constantly in order to keep him from becoming conceited.

"I was given a thorn in my flesh," he said, "a messenger of Satan, to torment me. Three times I pleaded with the Lord to take it away from me.

"But he said to me, 'My grace is sufficient for you, for my power is made perfect in weakness.'"[25]

Thank you for your grace in my suffering, Lord.

"Therefore I will boast all the more gladly about my weaknesses, so that Christ's power may rest on me.

"That is why, for Christ's sake, I delight in weaknesses, in insults, in hardships, in persecutions, in difficulties. For when I am weak, then I am strong,"[26] and secure in your arms.

---

[25] 2 Corinthians 12:7-9.
[26] Ibid. vv. 9-10.

day 12

Don't use words too big for the subject. Don't say "infinitely" when you mean "very"; otherwise you'll have no word left when you want to talk about something really infinite.[27]

I need you to help me improve my communication skills, Lord.

It's not that I can't spell or punctuate. I'm not a best-selling author, but I can write what I want to say. Writing isn't the problem.

The problem is when you give me a prophetic word for someone.

I communicate in so many ways—with my words, inflections, voice, posture, even my eyes. And they're all affected by my attitude.

Sometimes, for example, you're merely making a statement, but when it comes out of my mouth, it sounds like a judgment because of my attitude at the time.

---

[27] Dorsett, Lyle W.; Mead, Marjorie Lamp, editors, *C. S. Lewis' Letters to Children*, Letter to Joan Lancaster, 26 June 1956, Scribner, 3 June 1996.

23

Or, if not with my words, my posture may misrepresent you. I may not even realize that I'm leaning in toward somebody I'm talking to, and it makes you seem aggressive or hostile when you're not that at all.

The hardest thing, though, is when you give me an extensive word, but you don't want me to share it all. Sometimes, I'm tempted to share more than I should, thinking whoever's listening will be impressed that I know so much. But that doesn't sound like me. I don't really want that.

Teach me, Lord, how to distinguish between the thoughts in my head and the devil's voice in my ear.

More than that, teach me to recognize and delight in your voice.

day 13

Despair is only for those who see the end beyond all doubt. We do not.[28]

MOST of the time, when I reach one of those moments when I want to quit, it's because I think I know where what I'm doing is headed.

I think the road is just too long, or I think the fruit has already shriveled on the vine.

But I guess it would be more accurate to say that, when I reach one of those moments that I want to quit, it's because I think. Period.

Believing you is hard sometimes, because the objective is invisible or unimaginable, like being given a loaded rifle and told to hit a target I can neither see nor perceive.

Unbelief is a thorn in the side of the prophet, too.

---

[28] Tolkien, J. R. R., *The Fellowship of the Ring*, Houghton Mifflin Company, 1994.

"Did I really hear that? Did you really say that? What does it mean? That makes absolutely no sense to me. What are people going to think of me if I'm wrong?"

Thomas spent several years with you, watching you do impossible things, "and if every one of them were written down, I suppose that even the whole world would not have room for the books that would be written."[29]

You even raised Lazarus from the dead. And Thomas had witnessed it all. Yet, when he was told you had risen, he had to see to believe.

The need to see and understand will be a serious hindrance in the coming years. As you do things here on earth that have never been done before, many will fall away.

Hold me tight, Lord.

[29] John 21:25.

day 14

It's time for a new generation of revelatory people to arise.[30]

"MANY leaders have remained hidden in their closets of prayer, waiting on God to give them their promised ministry inheritance," said John Paul Jackson.

"They have waited for their character to become equal to or exceed the level of their gifting."[31]

How many of us have asked, "How long, Lord, are you going to let your church go on like this—asleep in its sanctuaries?"

That time is ending.

You're church is about to awaken, to see you as it has never seen you before and to become what it has never even imagined itself to be.

---

[30] Jackson, John Paul, *The Art of Hearing God*, Revised Sixth Edition, Streams Institute for Spiritual Development, 2010, p. 25.
[31] Ibid.

27

No one will remain on the fences, swaying between the world and the Lord. You're about to tear down the fences, and whichever way people are leaning at that moment is the side on which they will land.

More will run to you than ever before. Your church will become truly one, holy and glorious.

And we will hear your voice as never before.

"The intense pleasure you give me surpasses the gladness of harvest time, even more than when the harvesters gaze upon their ripened grain and when their new wine overflows.

"Now, because of you, Lord, I will lie down in peace and sleep comes at once, for no matter what happens, I will live unafraid!"[32]

---

[32] Psalm 4:7-8, TPT.

day 15

They bruised his feet with shackles, his neck was put in irons, till what he foretold came to pass, till the word of the Lord proved him true.[33]

PROPHECY isn't a name-it-and-claim-it gift or a magic act where a trumpeting pachyderm suddenly appears on an empty stage.

Your prophetic words reveal hidden sin, predict consequences and accomplish anything else you mean for them to do.

Often, prophecy gives direction, though not like a roadmap. I may not reach the turn you want me to take for a decade or two. And those decades may even seem to be moving me in the opposite direction.

In a couple of dreams, you told Joseph that his parents and brothers would bow before him.

---

[33] Psalm 105:18-19.

Instead, he was thrown into a pit, sold as a slave, hauled off to Egypt and imprisoned by the captain of Pharaoh's guard.

And yet, Joseph held unflinchingly to your promises.

I often experience what appears to be the death of a prophetic word while I'm still waiting for its fulfillment, and I find myself tempted by Despair.

But Joseph was eventually freed from prison and appointed ruler over all of Egypt. And when a widespread drought came, the dreams you had given him when he was seventeen were fulfilled.

Thank you, Lord, that you will always fulfill my prophecies, even though it might not happen in the way or time I expect.

Thank you for your plan for my life. And thank you most of all that it's built around you.

day 16

It is when we notice the dirt that God is most present in us; it is the very sign of His presence.[34]

IT'S hard sometimes to pray. Not because it interrupts my daily activities but because it brings me closer to you.

And often, when I move closer to you, when I see you a little more clearly, I become more acutely aware of how little we're alike.

Sometimes, I feel dirty in your presence, which sounds dirty even to say, but it's true. And somehow, you're okay with it. I'm the only one who has a problem.

I think it's Pride.

The closer I am to you, the purer or holier I think I am. I can't believe it's even possible for me to think like that when I'm standing before you.

[34] Lewis, Clive Staples, *The Collected Letters of C.S. Lewis*, Volume II, Harper San Francisco, 4 October 2005.

You reflect my image like a mirror, and I see my selfishness, how surprisingly dirty I am. And I know that should make me want more than anything to get clean. But it just makes me want to hide.

And that's usually when it happens.

You reach out to me, lift my chin and catch and hold my gaze.

And when I see the loving smile you give me, my dirtiness and ugliness don't seem to matter anymore. At least, I'm not aware of them anymore because I can no longer remember what I look like.

Your eyes are my only reality.

And that grin of yours . . .

Nobody ever warned me about that grin.

day 17

For as he thinks within himself, so he is.[35]

PROPHETS hang out with you a lot, which makes sense, because you're the source of our gift and call. But it's not out of gratitude or obligation.

I have an insatiable appetite for you. I just eat you up.

I'm not trying to get something from you. Not trying to summon words or insights to share. I'm fine if you don't speak at all (though I cherish the sound of your voice).

Sometimes, when you and I are together, we're a little like an old married couple, sitting together quietly in the living room. It's not that we have nothing to say to one another, and it's not that we sort of read one another's minds (which, of course, you do naturally). It's that we've just become so . . . "one," hanging out together.

---

[35] Proverbs 23:7, NASB.

33

When I sit with you, alone in the quiet, I know you. Not everything about you. That would be absurd, because you're, you know, God.

There's just a unity between us that we both enjoy.

Maybe that's why you share things with me. You've made me sort of an extension of you.

You're like that with all your children, even though not all of your children have learned to be like that with you.

You want to reveal yourself to us, because you long to be fully known by us. Because you want us to understand you and experience unity with you.

Because you're Love, and you made us one with you.

day 18

*For prophecy never had its origin in the human
will, but prophets, though human, spoke from
God as they were carried along by the Holy
Spirit.*[36]

PROPHECY is all about faith.
And faith is all about
relationship.

The prophet Moses had an ongoing
relationship with you. He had faith to
argue with a blazing bush, to go head
to head with Pharaoh and to call forth
a dozen plagues. His faith carried him
out of Egypt, across the Red Sea and
through the desert to Kadesh.

There, however, he ignored your
instructions and eventually died on
Mount Nebo, never entering the land
he was promised.

This is why prophets spend so
much time alone with you. To speak
for you, we have to recognize, not only
your voice, but also your character.

---

[36] 2 Peter 1:21.

Prophecy is not merely a matter of what we hear but of distinguishing your voice from all the voices buzzing in and around us.

But recognizing your voice is not enough either.

We have to understand your nature, who you are and why you would do the things you tell us you're going to do.

We need to know you as Love, not as Lawmaker or Punisher.

I want to know *you*, Lord, not just things about you. To understand love and how it motivates you.

To learn to love and be motivated like you.

I want to recognize your voice, no matter where or when you speak.

I want to feel your heart as it beats next to mine.

day 19

"Leave here, turn eastward and hide in the Kerith Ravine, east of the Jordan. You will drink from the brook, and I have directed the ravens to supply you with food there."[37]

"THE truly spiritual man is indeed something of an oddity…. His joy is to see his Lord promoted and himself neglected.

"He finds few who care to talk about that which is the supreme object of his interest, so he is often silent and preoccupied in the midst of noisy religious shoptalk."[38]

Your prophets have chosen between you and the world, not merely whether or not to be Christians but with whom we will spend the majority of our lives.

Having selected you, my mind delights in your thoughts and character

---

[37] 1 Kings 17:3-4.
[38] Tozer, A.W., *Man: the Dwelling Place of God*, Moody Bible Institute of Chicago, 1966, p. 96.

rather than with the changing trends and character of the culture that surrounds me.

We respond to a worldly church by cleansing it, not condemning it, "consumed with a fiery passion to keep your house pure" as you cleansed your Father's house when you saw it "filled with merchants selling oxen, lambs, and doves for exorbitant prices, while others were overcharging as they exchanged currency behind their counters."[39]

Distract me, Lord.

Hold my gaze while I breathe deeply of your love for me.

Enable me to recognize the inconsequence of the attractions of the world that I have so often and so foolishly preferred to you.

---

[39] John 3:14, 17, TPT.

day 20

And as Jesus rose up out of the water, the heavenly realm opened up over him and he saw the Holy Spirit descend out of the heavens and rest upon him in the form of a dove.[40]

YOU'RE not a bird.

You're God, the triune God, not merely one of three interchangeable gods who rule as called upon.

But that's about as far as I can go with the Trinity thing. It's totally beyond my ability to understand.

I do know, though, that you rule everything down here and empower me to do astounding things that began with repentance (I'll never get why I said yes to salvation and people just like me say no. It's insane. If they'd just take a few minutes to consider the consequences. . . . But I guess they don't believe in the consequences either.)

---

[40] Matthew 3:16, TPT.

And that's as much as I can think about that.

I also know that you teach and heal and comfort. You're truth and life, holiness and glory. You're my defender and my champion.

You sacrificed more than I can possibly understand for me, and you have prepared, and will continue to prepare, more for me than I can ever conceive of properly appreciating.

And Prophet to prophet, you reveal your wonders to me. You're the thoughts I think, the voice I hear, the image I see.

You're the toucher and breaker and re-maker of my heart.

Nothing and no one can be even remotely compared to you.

And there's no one and nothing I'd rather chase after than you, my Love.

day 21

But when they arrest you and deliver you up, do not worry beforehand, or premeditate what you will speak. But whatever is given you in that hour, speak that; for it is not you who speak, but the Holy Spirit.[41]

PROPHECY is a gift. You gave it to build us up in our rip-it-all-apart world.

Your sweet voice, Holy Spirit, calls us out of our selfishness and comforts us in our failures and our sufferings.

"Do not yield to fear in the face of the suffering to come," you caution, ". . . but remain faithful to the day you die and I will give you the victor's crown of life."[42]

You prophetically confirm our spiritual destiny.

"Who do you say I am?" you asked Simon Peter.

"You are the Christ," he replied, "the Son of the living God."

---

[41] Mark 13:11, NKJV.
[42] Revelation 2:10, TPT.

Then you prophesied: "I tell you that you are Peter, and on this rock I will build my church, and the gates of Hades will not overcome it.

"I will give you the keys of the kingdom of heaven; whatever you bind on earth will be bound in heaven, and whatever you loose on earth will be loosed in heaven."[43]

Prophecy brushes away lies to reveal truth and turns mustard-seeds into mountains.

Have I thanked you recently for this rich gift, Lord?

Have I thanked you for any of your gifts?

Forgive me for taking them for granted, for picking and choosing which I will use and when, if at all.

[43] Matthew 16:16, 18-19.

day 22

For he knew all about us before we were born and he destined us from the beginning to share the likeness of his Son. This means the Son is the oldest among a vast family of brothers and sisters who will become just like him.[44]

PAUL prophesied that when you appear, we'll be like you, because we'll see you as you are. And with this hope, we can purify ourselves.[45]

So, it's really been possible for a couple thousand years for us to become pure, like you, here on this sinful, polluted old planet?

I looked it up, and *purify* means to make clear, to free from pollution. Doesn't seem possible down here.

Then again, you 're the Miracle Worker, right? And I was reborn and remade in your likeness.

So, I'm not just an old sinner saved by grace. I'm your presence on earth,

---

44 Romans 8:29, TPT.
45 1 John 3:2-3.

which makes sin optional for me, just as it was for Adam in Eden.

Of course, I'll still make mistakes. I mean you made lots of mistakes when you were growing up with Joseph and Mary, didn't you? But mistakes aren't necessarily sins.

Wow! It might take some time for me to get my head around that.

I guess it's a little like a perfect rose garden. It doesn't have *flawless* roses. It has *only* roses. No weeds, daffodils or critters.

Thank you for giving me the power to have a weedless, critterless garden … and to become more like you, here and now, than I ever imagined.

Watch out for false prophets. They come to you in sheep's clothing, but inwardly they are ferocious wolves.[46]

YOU taught me that a prophet who gets it wrong isn't necessarily a false prophet.

I used to worry about that when I first learned about prophecy and was wrestling up the courage to try it.

But false prophets don't worry about being wrong. They delight in it, because they're liars, plotters and deceivers, constantly on the hunt for victims.

Because a prophet is false, however, doesn't mean his gift isn't real. He can prophesy accurately, and an undiscerning person can take that as evidence that the false prophet is the real deal.

Fruit is only reliable test.

---

[46] Matthew 7:15.

"Every good tree bears good fruit," you said, "but a bad tree bears bad fruit." No exceptions.

A good tree isn't even capable of bearing bad fruit. "Thus, by their fruit you will recognize them."

Then, you said something else that can keep me awake at night.

"Every tree that does not bear good fruit is cut down and thrown into the fire."[47]

You weren't talking about trees, and you weren't talking about fire.

Being burned alive is a horrible way to execute somebody. I think of Hugh Latimer and Nicholas Ridley and Joan of Arc. At least death ended their agonies.

Hell, on the other hand, is suffering without end.

It bothers me less, though, the closer I move toward you, my Love.

---

[47] Ibid. vv. 16-20.

day 24

"I the Lord do not change."[48]

WHEN you were here with us in the flesh and even today, you said a lot of things that left people scratching their heads.

There were all those odd parables about wheat and tares and leaven and mustard seeds, lost sheep and lost coins, pearls and prodigals.

And once, when your disciples were rebuking people who were pressing in with babies to bless, you said anyone who will not receive the kingdom of God like a little child will never enter it. Huh?

Another time, you said it's easier for a camel to go through the eye of a needle than for a rich man to enter your kingdom, which again left everybody scratching their heads.

You seem to be doing the same thing with your prophets today. You

---

[48] Malachi 3:6.

give us a word to share that seems to mean nothing. We share it, and somebody bursts into tears. Or you give us what sounds like a pretty clear word, and the person just shrugs his shoulders and walks away.

Being a prophet can be frightening and frustrating sometimes. There's always that awareness that, if you say nothing, I have nothing to say.

Then, there are the times when you say something and I'm not sure if it's you, who it's for or what it means in case they ask.

Fortunately, that was mostly back in the beginning, when I was so aware of myself.

The more I hang out with you, the less the uncertainties bother me.

And you never judge me or demand anything from me. You just always seem to be happy to be here in my awareness.

day 25

The prophet Zechariah spoke God's judgment against Judah. And "they plotted against him, and by order of the king they stoned him to death in the courtyard of the Lord's temple."[49]

PROPHETS are sought after and loved when they prophesy what people want to hear. When they don't, they aren't.

"Woe to you," you warned, "when all men speak well of you, for so did their fathers to the false prophets."[50]

But the problem doesn't seem to be between people and prophets. It seems to be between people and you.

Many people today are still idolaters. But we don't fashion idols out of gold, we fashion idols out of wishes.

We look for religious leaders who portray you as our loving God, then redefine you. Love would never say

---

49 2 Chronicles 24:20-21.
50 Luke 6:26.

anything hurtful, they say. So your rebukes prove you're not our God.

Love would always heal the sick, they say. So when the sick don't get healed, again, you're not our God.

Love, they say, isn't biased. So when you release someone to the devil to learn the lesson he needs in order to repent,[51] you prove again that you can't be our God.

Our problem is not Pride. Our problem is Stupidity.

We fashion idols and then work hard to make ourselves believe that they're you. And the longer we believe in them, the more real they become, until we wouldn't recognize you if you walked in the front door.

I know that idols have tempted stronger people than me, Lord. So I'll play it safe and keep my eyes fixed tightly on you.

---

[51] 1 Corinthians 5:1-5.

day 26

*Joy, by the grace of God, is the transfiguration
of suffering into endurance, and of endurance
into character, and of character into hope—
and the hope that has become our joy does not
disappoint us.*[52]

HAPPINESS can't stand pain.
So we do whatever it takes to
nurture or revive it.

But why? What is happiness?

America's first dictionary writer
defined it as "the agreeable sensations
which spring from the enjoyment of
good,"[53] like a belch after steak and ale,
I guess.

What a piddly, insignificant thing
happiness seems!

Maybe that's why the word doesn't
appear even once in the Bible. And
"happy" shows up only twenty-six

---

[52] Wangerin Jr., Walter, *Reliving the Passion*,
Zondervan, 7 March 1992.
[53] Webster, Noah, American Dictionary of the
English Language, 1828, p. 97.

times, one of which reads, "Happy is the man whom God corrects."[54]

"Therefore," says the rest of that verse, "do not despise the chastening of the Almighty."

Correction and chastening don't sound much like the happiness everybody's always talking about.

Then again, we all make corrections on the job, on our way to unfamiliar destinations, in our marriages—all the time. Because corrections are made to make things better.

Thank you, Lord, for all your loving corrections.

Thank you for your unwillingness to leave me as I am or to let me continue in the directions my flesh wants to go.

Thank you for letting me delight in the delicious superiority of joy over happiness.

---

[54] Job 5:17, NKJV.

day 27

Becoming fearless isn't the point. That's impossible. It's learning how to control your fear, and how to be free from it.[55]

"LOVE will find its way through paths where wolves would fear to prey."[56]

I've got it, Lord. Love is the only thing stronger than fear. Not courage. Not weapons. Not superior strength. Love.

Life down here is dangerous. Maybe not as dangerous as in the Middle Ages, with Black Death that killed half of Europe, famine, robbers and Holy Wars, but dangerous nonetheless.

And people are afraid—of corrupt government officials[57] and pollution, of

---

[55] Roth, Veronica, *Divergent*, Katherine Tegen Books, 30 September 2014.
[56] Byron, George Gordon, *The Giaour*, 1813, No. 51.
[57] The Chapman University Survey of American Fears Wave 5 (2018). This was the fourth year in a

53

running out of money in the future, serious illness and dying, of global warming and high medical bills.

I'm not saying that things aren't bad here, Lord.

The world since Eden is filled, not only with sickness, disease and tragedies but with people who commit indescribable atrocities against other people.

Nevertheless, I love you because you are my salvation. I can always trust you and need never be afraid, because you are my strength and my defense.[58]

My flesh and my heart may fail, but you are the strength of my heart and my portion forever.[59]

Thank you.

---

row that nearly three out of four people said they were most afraid of corrupt government officials.
[58] Isaiah 12:2.
[59] Psalm 73:26.

day 28

Nevertheless, I have this against you: You tolerate that woman Jezebel, who calls herself a prophet. By her teaching she misleads my servants into sexual immorality and the eating of food sacrificed to idols.[60]

THE prophetic is a spiritual realm where your prophets live, but not with you and your angels alone.

Demons are here. And the one that plagued Elijah through King Ahab's wife, Jezebel, appears to be assigned permanently to destroy every one of your prophets.[61]

The death of Jezebel might be encouraging if it was also the end of her demon. But it wasn't. And it won't stop coming after your prophets until you settle with it.

In the meantime, though, I don't have to worry about it, because the

---

[60] Revelation 2:20.
[61] 1 Kings 16, 18-19, 21; 2 Kings 9; Revelation 2.

Jezebel demon and all its associates have no choice but to submit to me in your name.[62]

I need fear nothing here on earth or in the spirit world.

In every situation—by prayer and petition, with thanksgiving—I need only present my requests to you, and your peace will protect my heart and mind.[63]

Everything here on earth is about hanging out with you.

When I don't, I'm just a victim of the Fall. When I do, I paint a target on my back, but you surround me with an impenetrable hedge of protection.

That doesn't mean I'm safe from persecution or martyrdom. It means that, as long as I hang tight with you, the worst that can be done to me down here on earth will merely set me free and send me home to you.

---

[62] Luke 10:17.
[63] Philippians 4:6-7.

day 29

I think it would be worse to expect nothing than to be disappointed.[64]

YOUR Bible is filled with promises. So, naturally, I have expectations, which is good. But it's also where the troubles begin.

I too often anticipate, rather than expect. I read your promises in the light of my circumstances, and I not only expect you to act in a certain way but also anticipate what and when and how you'll act, as though we share the same limitations, which is ridiculous, but I do it.

Of course, I suffer disappointment, because "hope deferred makes the heart sick."[65]

That's because my expectations and timing are rarely yours. Yours are better . . . okay, perfect.

---

[64] Montgomery, Lucy Maud, *Anne of Green Gables*, Anne Shirley to Aunt Marilla, June 1908.
[65] Proverbs 13:12.

Disappointment isn't a sin. But it's a doorway that can lead me to discouragement, which will lead me on to disillusionment, depression and unbelief.

And then, I've got sin.

It's all about trust, I suppose.

Trust isn't a matter of believing what you say, because we often misinterpret or misunderstand you.

Trust is a matter of believing who you are—understanding that you are Truth, so you can't deceive me, and you are Love, so you wouldn't deceive me.

In short, you are God, and there is no deception in you.

Would you remind me of all of this from time to time?

It will help me keep my eyes off your promises, the clock and my circumstances and keep them glued to you.

day 30

"And then alas! I let the matter reset, watching and waiting only, as we have too often done." [66]

WAITING is the hardest thing I do as a Christian. For that matter, it was the hardest thing to do before I even knew you. And I didn't do it often, I can tell you.

Waiting is especially difficult for me when you're silent. You don't tell me when I'm supposed to start waiting, how long I'll have to wait or when I should stop waiting and start doing something. I call, and your phone just keeps ringing. And when the ringing stops, everything is silent again, and the silence is enough to drive me nuts.

Sometimes, I quit waiting. I figure (or rationalize) that because I haven't heard from you, you aren't involved, and I needn't be either.

[66] Tolkein, J.R.R., *The Fellowship of the Ring*, George Allen & Unwin, 1954.

Unfortunately, waiting on you is the defining discipline of the prophet. It's a continuing conflict between soul and spirit, smashing warped philosophies, tearing down barriers erected against your truth, fitting every loose thought and emotion and impulse into the structure of the life you've shaped for me.[67]

And it gets harder when I remember that waiting doesn't even guarantee that I'm going to live to see what I'm waiting for.

Sometimes I just need to get that off my chest before I get back to waiting.

And waiting isn't really all that bad, because all the time I'm waiting, I'm with you, even if I'm doing all the talking, like now.

---

[67] 2 Corinthians 10:5-6, MSG.

RON CAMPBELL

 Born in South Africa, Ron was led by the Holy Spirit to America in 1993 to minister life and transformation in the office of a prophet. He is used powerfully by the Lord, ministering healing and building up believers through his prophetic gift.

Ron's clients include the Texas legislature, U.S. Senate and House of Representatives, and Life Care Medical Foundation, as well as oil corporations, technology companies, churches and nongovernment organizations.

Ron is also a popular and engaging conference, seminar and keynote speaker.

Sound the Trumpet Publications
PO Box 188
Grapevine, TX 76099
www.soundthetrumpet.org

RON BRACKIN

An investigative journalist, Ron is the author of more than 25 books, including the international bestseller, *Son of Hama*s.

In Washington, D. C., he served as a broadcast journalist with the all-news CBS radio station and as a congressional press secretary during the Reagan Administration.

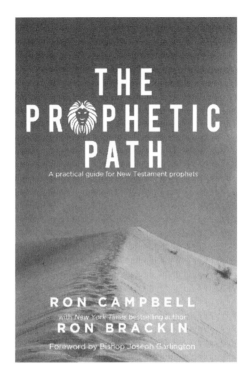

THE
PROPHETIC
PATH

A practical guide for New Testament prophets

RON CAMPBELL
with *New York Times* bestselling author
RON BRACKIN

Foreword by Bishop Joseph Garlington

The Prophetic Path is a powerful discipleship resource, not only for emerging prophets but for all who would be prophetic.

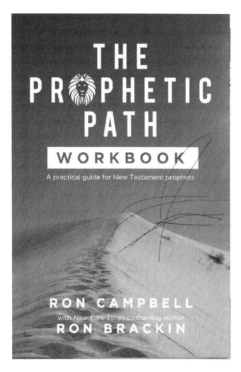

The Prophetic Path Workbook picks up where The Prophetic Path leaves off and takes emerging prophets farther and deeper into the prophetic.

Made in the USA
Middletown, DE
18 January 2022